Palenque

UNEARTHING ANCIENT WORLDS

Deborah Kops

Twenty-First Century Books • Minneapolis

For my mother-in-law, Inez Covell, with love

Twenty-First Century Books
A division of Lerner Publishing Group, Inc.
241 First Avenue North
Minneapolis, MN 55401 U.S.A.

Website address: www.lernerbooks.com

Library of Congress Cataloging-in-Publication Data

Kops, Deborah.
    Palenque / by Deborah Kops.
        p.   cm. — (Unearthing ancient worlds)
    Includes bibliographical references and index.
    ISBN 978–0–8225–7504–7 (lib. bdg. : alk. paper)
    1. Palenque Site (Mexico)—Juvenile literature. 2. Mayas—Mexico—Palenque (Chiapas)—Antiquities—Juvenile literature. 3. Excavations (Archaeology)—Mexico—Palenque (Chiapas)—Juvenile literature. 4. Palenque (Chiapas, Mexico)—Antiquities—Juvenile literature. I. Title.
F1435.1.P2K66 2008
972'.75—dc22   2007021323

Manufactured in the United States of America
1 2 3 4 5 6 – PA – 13 12 11 10 09 08

TABLE OF CONTENTS

The rain forest surrounds the remains of the ancient Mayan city of Palenque, built around A.D. 600 in present-day southern Mexico. Archaeologists have been using clues from this and other ancient Mayan cities to try to understand how the ancient Maya lived and what caused their surprising disappearance.

INTRODUCTION

About fifteen hundred years ago, Palenque was one of the Mayan civilization's most beautiful cities. It perched on a terrace in the rugged mountains of what became southern Mexico. A lush tropical forest surrounded the city.

The name *Palenque* means "steep cliffs." The mountain peaks shot up more than 2,000 feet (610 meters) above Palenque's terrace. About 600 feet (183 m) below stretched a great plain, where many Mayan people lived in simple wooden houses and grew corn.

The terrace overlooking the cornfields was the ceremonial center of Palenque. The royal family lived there in a grand, sprawling palace with a square tower. The palace and the airy, elegant temples on the terrace were made of stone, which the Maya painted dark red. They built an aqueduct to bring water to the palace from a nearby river.

The finest temple on the terrace honored Pakal, the king of Palenque from A.D. 615 to 683. Pakal spent the last eight years of his long life supervising the construction of this temple, which was near his palace. When Pakal's workers finished building the temple, he had them mount three stone tablets on its walls. Two were huge—about 13 feet (4 m) high—and one was smaller. On these tablets, scribes engraved in hieroglyphs (picture

This stucco sculpture of the head of Mayan king Pakal was found in his tomb beneath the Temple of the Inscriptions.

writing) the important events of Pakal's reign and the history of his family.

Pakal's temple sat on top of a tall pyramid. Deep inside the pyramid was a tomb where Pakal wanted to be buried. It held a large stone coffin with a heavy limestone lid. The coffin was painted red inside, and its lid was carved with Pakal's portrait. The picture shows him falling into the underworld, where the lords of death ruled.

When Pakal finally died at the age of eighty, his subjects buried him according to ancient Mayan rituals. His oldest son, Chan Bahlum, probably took charge. To get to the coffin, Chan Bahlum and his younger brother, Kan Xul, climbed the pyramid and entered the temple. Then they descended a long stairway to the inside of the pyramid's base. They laid Pakal on his back in the coffin. On his chest, they placed a large piece of jewelry made from 189 gleaming, tube-shaped beads. The beads were made of jade, a dark green stone that was very precious to the Maya. The

men placed a magnificent jade mask, which looked like Pakal, on his face.

Chan Bahlum, Kan Xul, and two other men put a smooth stone cover on the coffin. Then workers lifted the heavy carved slab onto the coffin. It was a hard, sweaty job.

One very difficult task remained. The Maya believed they had to sacrifice some people so Pakal's soul could be reborn as an ancestor in the sky world. It was probably Chan Bahlum and other relatives who killed six young people and put the bodies in a stone box near Pakal's coffin.

A modern-day artist depicts what a Mayan nobleman's funeral may have looked like. The deceased lies in the tomb *(below left)* surrounded by food and drink for the afterlife, while servants stack stones to seal the tomb. A priest in ceremonial dress *(above right)* recites prayers, and a captive is prepared for sacrifice. The dead nobleman's widow in white robes and jade *(top center)*, along with warriors and friends, attends the ceremony.

FAST FACTS ABOUT PALENQUE

- During the Classical period (A.D. 292 to 909), the ancient Maya lived in modern-day southern Mexico, Belize, Guatemala, and Honduras.

- The Maya may have founded the city of Palenque as early as 100 B.C., but they built most of the buildings that still stand between A.D. 600 and 760.

- The greatest ruler of Palenque, Pakal, became king in A.D. 615, when he was only twelve years old.

- Most of the great buildings in Palenque, including the palace, were built during Pakal's reign.

- No new buildings were constructed after the late A.D. 700s. By A.D. 800, Palenque was deserted. Nobody knows why.

- In 1524 the Spanish conqueror of Mexico, Hernán Cortés, came within thirty miles (48 kilometers) of Palenque but didn't know it.

Soon after Pakal's funeral, Chan Bahlum became king. One of the first things he did as king was finish the temple honoring his father. On the square columns in front, he added pictures of Pakal and of himself as a child. These pictures were stucco sculptures painted red, yellow, and blue. Each one showed Pakal choosing Chan Bahlum to become Palenque's next ruler.

About a century after Pakal's death, the Maya left Palenque. The city was empty by A.D. 800. The Maya abandoned all their other nearby cities too. No one is sure why.

Eventually, most people forgot the ancient Maya. Jungle trees choked their glorious temples and palaces. By the time an American explorer and a British architect visited Palenque in 1840, the world seemed to have forgotten that the ancient Maya had ever existed.

Sites of the
Ancient Maya

Chichén
Itzá ▲

Uxmal ▲
▲ Sayil

Tulum ▲

*Gulf of
Mexico*

N
W E
S

Altun
Ha
▲

▲ Palenque

Uaxactún ▲

BELIZE

MEXICO

Yaxchilán
▲

Tikal
▲

▲ Toniná

Caracol
▲

*Caribbean
Sea*

Bonampak
▲

▲ Seibal

GUATEMALA

Quiriguá ▲

Miles
0   25   50   75   100
0   50   100   150
Kilometers

▲ Copán

HONDURAS

*PACIFIC
OCEAN*

▲ Archaeological site
-·- Modern border

EL SALVADOR

Stephens and Catherwood's journey to Palenque covered thousands of miles through the
wilderness of Honduras and Mexico. All of the equipment and supplies had to be carried

CHAPTER one

STEPHENS TELLS THE WORLD

Early one morning in May 1840, John Stephens and Frederick Catherwood ride their mules through the jungle in southern Mexico. Finally, they will see Palenque! They are not alone. One of the local residents—Stephens and Catherwood call them Indians—guides them. Other Indians help them carry their supplies, including Catherwood's stacks of drawing paper. He is an architect, and he plans to make detailed pictures and architectural plans of the ancient buildings.

The Indians are also carrying food for Stephens and Catherwood, who will camp at the ruins. One has a live turkey strapped to his back. Another carries a string of eggs, wrapped carefully in banana leaves and tied together with strips of bark.

John Stephens, an American, has been waiting for this moment for a long time. When he was back home in New York, he had read some visitors' accounts of the mysterious ruins in Mexico and Central America. He just *had* to see them for himself. Although he is an American lawyer and a diplomat, he certainly does not look like one.

U.S. president Martin van Buren appointed John Stephens (*above*) as a special ambassador to Central America in 1839.

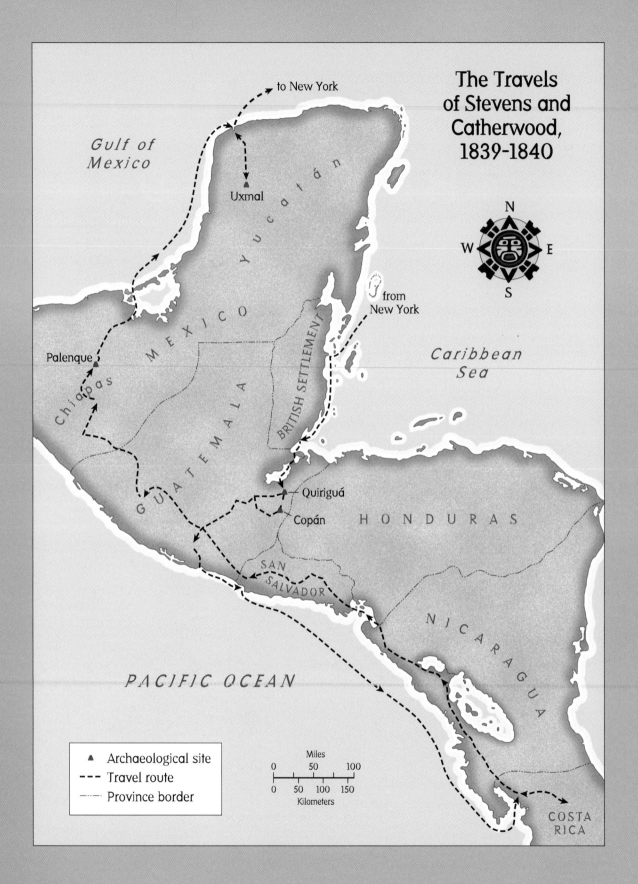

The Travels of Stevens and Catherwood, 1839-1840

to New York

Gulf of Mexico

Uxmal

Yucatán

Palenque

Chiapas

MEXICO

GUATEMALA

BRITISH SETTLEMENT

from New York

Caribbean Sea

N
W E
S

Quiriguá

Copán

HONDURAS

SAN SALVADOR

NICARAGUA

PACIFIC OCEAN

▲ Archaeological site
--- Travel route
-·-·- Province border

Miles
0   50   100
0   50   100   150
Kilometers

COSTA RICA

He and Catherwood wear native clothing, including large hats and in rainy weather, goatskin to keep them dry.

Stephens and Catherwood are exhausted. They've been exploring the region's deserted ruins for months. They've traveled thousands of miles along narrow trails through the jungles and hills of Honduras and Mexico.

In Honduras they visited the ancient city of Copán. It was filled with pyramids. The stone statues there were twice as tall as the men. The two explorers also saw hieroglyphs that didn't look at all like the glyphs they'd seen in Egypt.

Stephens and Catherwood's journey has been tiring, but it has also sharpened their curiosity. What will they find at Palenque?

This sculpture, called a stela, is one of many Stephens and Catherwood would have encountered while traveling through the ancient Mayan city of Copán in modern-day Honduras. Archaeologists have since discovered that the Maya carved these statues to record important dates and to note events in rulers' lives.

A PALACE FOR BATS AND FIREFLIES

The trail through the jungle is muddy. After the party has traveled a few hours, the trail grows so steep that the mules make very slow progress. Stephens, Catherwood, and the Indians climb onto a terrace. Suddenly some Indians cry out.

This view of Palenque is as it appeared when Stephens, Catherwood, and their guide found it in 1840. Catherwood made dozens of drawings of their findings at Palenque. Later, he made full-color paintings like this one based on his sketches.

Through an opening in the trees, the two explorers see a large stone building the color of sand. Square columns support what is left of the crumbling roof. Gigantic images of people with long, flat faces decorate the columns. In the middle of the building stands a four-story square tower.

Trees grow against the palace walls, and their branches enter some of its fourteen doorways. The ruin strikes Stephens as both sad and beautiful.

Stephens and Catherwood run up the stone steps of the palace. To celebrate their arrival, they fire off four rounds with their guns. Stephens has another reason for shooting his gun too. He hopes the Indians will tell everyone in the nearby town that he and Catherwood have weapons. If word gets around, no one will try to disturb them.

Their noise bothers three large fruit bats, which begin circling the ruined palace. As the bats fly overhead, Stephens and Catherwood investigate the building. It is a maze of hallways and high-ceilinged rooms arranged around four courtyards.

Although the palace will not give the explorers much shelter from rain, they decide to stay there. They bring their turkey, their mules, and some chickens up the steps and let the animals loose in a courtyard. The Indians prepare to leave. They do not want to stay at the

The palace at Palenque was built on a base that is 300 feet (91 m) by 240 feet (73 m). The tower stands four stories high.

The palace courtyard provided an enclosed space where Stephens and Catherwood kept their mules and livestock.

ruins at night. Some promise to return with fresh milk the next morning.

By late afternoon, Stephens and Catherwood are settled in. As they enjoy their dinner outside, the sky blackens. They hear a loud clap of thunder. A strong gust of wind whips through the trees. Torrents of rain follow, forcing the men to run into the palace. It rains every afternoon at this time of year.

Inside the palace, fireflies longer than 0.5 inch (1.3 centimeters) light up the hallway where the men are staying. In the strange light, stucco sculptures on the palace walls seem to come alive. There are stucco snakes. And there are soldiers whose heads have worn away over the centuries.

Many insects, unlike the fireflies, are not helpful at all. Swarms of mosquitoes make it hard to sleep. The chigoes are the worst. These tiny

"By the light of a single [firefly] we read distinctly the finely-printed pages of an American newspaper . . . and it seemed stranger than any incident on my journey to be reading by the light of beetles, in the ruined palace of Palenque, the sayings and doings of great men at home."

—John Stephens, 1853

burrowing fleas lay their eggs under Stephens's toenails and make his foot swell.

Catherwood spends days making architectural floor plans and drawings of the palace. The floor plans show the locations and shapes of all the

Frederick Catherwood's exquisite paintings of Palenque, including this painting of the palace, give modern viewers an idea of what the site looked like long ago, when it had lain hidden in the jungle for so many years.

rooms and hallways. He also draws the stucco sculptures that are in the best condition. In one of them, a man with a flattened head stands proudly. He is wearing a headdress with feathers and other decorations. Stephens helps by cleaning off the objects that Catherwood wants to draw.

Mayan Beauty

Mayan kings and noble people wanted to have long, flat foreheads like the maize god, one of their most important gods. Parents tied two boards to their baby's head—one in front and one in back—to lengthen and flatten the skull.

This relief portrait of a Mayan woman shows her flattened forehead, elaborate hairdo, and facial tatoos—all signs of beauty in ancient Mayan culture.

To make his drawings, Catherwood uses a tool called a camera lucida. He points the camera at the object he wants to draw. He lays a sheet of paper on a hard surface beneath the camera. When he looks into the camera, he sees the image he wants to draw as if it is already on the paper. Catherwood traces around the image. The camera helps him draw very detailed pictures. When he wants to draw very tall objects, he builds a high platform and works on top of it with his camera.

THE MYSTERIOUS GLYPHS

The men find much to explore in the ruined palace. Stephens notices a stone aqueduct next to the palace. Because of all the rain, water flows over its sides.

One day Stephens decides to climb the palace tower. Looking to the southwest, he sees a building on top of a pyramid. He invites Catherwood to

When Stephens climbed to the top of the palace tower *(right)*, he was able to see a building on top of a stepped pyramid *(left)*.

investigate it with him. They quickly cut their way through the jungle growth with the help of their Indian guide.

The two explorers and the guide slowly climb the steep steps leading up one side of the pyramid. It is about 70 feet (21 m) tall. When they reach the building at the top, they notice stucco sculptures of people on four of its six square columns. The people's faces have worn off, but Stephens and Catherwood see an adult and a child on each column. Traces of red, yellow, and blue paint remain all over the stucco.

This is a close-up of one of the stucco columns supporting the building at the top of the pyramid. It shows a standing person wearing noble headgear and holding a scepter with two seated people at his feet. The paint has faded over the years and is barely visible in this photograph.

After climbing the steep stairs leading to the top of the pyramid, Stephens and Catherwood saw that the building on top had these four beautifully carved columns.

Stephens can't figure out the purpose of this building. He calls it simply *casa de piedras*, or "stone house." And since Palenque contains other stone buildings, he calls this stone house number one.

The three men enter the building, and the guide cries out in surprise. He points to two moss-covered stone tablets about 13 feet (4 m) high. The men quickly scrape off the moss with sticks to see what lies beneath it. Hundreds of carved glyphs fill the tablets.

The explorers can see the neatly arranged symbols on one tablet clearly. Some symbols have human or animal faces. Others look like clusters of squiggly lines. Dots and dashes are everywhere.

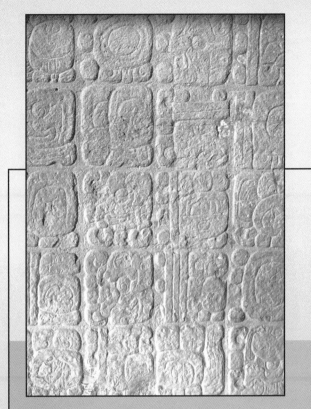

Stephens and Catherwood
discovered three stone tablets such
as this one covered with glyphs.

> "The intermediate country [between Copán and Palenque] is now occupied by races of Indians speaking many different languages . . . but there is room for the belief that the whole of this country was once occupied by the same race, speaking the same language, or at least, having the same written characters."
>
> —John Stephens, 1853

Centuries of wind and rain have worn away half the writing on the other tablet. But the men notice on the temple's back wall a third, smaller tablet with still more glyphs. This tablet's location has protected it from the weather, and it is in perfect condition.

The men light candles so Catherwood can copy the complex symbols. Other travelers may have visited this building before them, but no one has ever drawn these glyphs. Catherwood copies them with great care. Stephens notices that they are very similar to the glyphs in Copán. He is sure they are important. He calls them "the real written records of a lost people."

Next, Stephens and Catherwood measure the building carefully so Catherwood can produce an accurate floor plan. Catherwood also copies the four tall stucco figures on the building's front columns. His drawings show them exactly as he sees them, with heads or arms missing.

The men wonder: Who built this amazing city? When did they live here? No one knows, because no one has figured out how to read their hieroglyphs. About twenty years earlier, a man had finally figured out how to read ancient Egyptian hieroglyphs. Who would decode the tablets at Palenque?

As May wears on, Stephens and Catherwood find it more and more difficult to work. They have discovered more buildings and pyramids, and Catherwood has drawn them all. They do not sleep well, though. The afternoon rains are growing heavier. On June 1,

Below is a Catherwood painting of one Palenque's many buildings. Stephens and Catherwood called this building Casa (house) no. 3.

1840, they leave Palenque. On June 24, they board a ship bound for Cuba. There they will catch another boat to New York.

STRANDED IN THE CARIBBEAN SEA

Stephens and Catherwood's journey comes to a sudden halt in the middle of the Caribbean Sea. This sea is near the equator. Equatorial waters often lack enough wind to push a sailing ship. The men's ship sits for days on an ocean as calm as glass. By July 13, their drinking water has run out. Sharks circle the boat menacingly.

> "I had but one leave-taking, and that was a trying one. I was to bid farewell to my noble [mule]. He had carried me more than two thousand miles [3,200 km], over the worst road that mule ever traveled. . . . I threw my arms around his neck. His eyes had a mournful expression."
>
> —John Stephens, 1853

Eventually the wind begins to blow, but it is not strong enough to move the ship. Stephens begins to wonder whether he and Catherwood will die. His notes and Catherwood's drawings will float away. No one will learn about their discoveries.

Just when the end seems near, another ship sails into view. When it gets close enough, Stephens calls out. The sailors on the ship, called the *Helen Maria*, pull Stephens, Catherwood, and their belongings aboard. The *Helen Maria* sails better in light winds. It takes them all the way to New York, where they land on July 31.

STEPHENS WRITES A BEST SELLER

The following spring, Stephens finishes writing a long book on his adventures with Catherwood. He calls it *Incidents of Travel in Central*

This title page is from John Stephens's book *Incidents of Travel in Central America, Chiapas, and Yucatan*. In the second volume, he discusses his visit to Palenque. Catherwood provided the many illustrations.

INCIDENTS OF TRAVEL

IN

CENTRAL AMERICA, CHIAPAS,

AND

YUCATAN.

BY JOHN L. STEPHENS,

AUTHOR OF "INCIDENTS OF TRAVEL IN EGYPT, ARABIA PETRÆA, AND THE
HOLY LAND," ETC.

ILLUSTRATED BY NUMEROUS ENGRAVINGS.

IN TWO VOLUMES.

VOL. I.

LONDON:
JOHN MURRAY, ALBEMARLE STREET.
MDCCCXLI.

America, Chiapas, and Yucatan. It is filled with Catherwood's fine drawings of all they've seen, including the three tablets of glyphs at Palenque.

The book is very popular. The famous author Edgar Allan Poe declares that it might be the most interesting travel book ever written. Scholars argue about who built Palenque and the other ruins that Stephens and Catherwood visited. They wonder if the people came from Europe, Asia, or North Africa.

Many readers notice the similarity between Mexican and Egyptian pyramids. They wonder whether the ancestors of the people who built Palenque were Egyptians. Stephens points out that the pyramid was a logical form for early builders. It provides both a strong foundation and great height.

Stephens also notes some important differences between the architecture of Palenque and ancient Egypt. The ancient Egyptians built temples with massive columns that were much wider than the columns in Palenque. The Egyptians also created avenues approaching their temples, while the builders of Palenque did not. Stephens concludes there simply isn't enough evidence to link the people who lived in Palenque with the ancient Egyptians. He is sure the ancient residents of Palenque were not from Egypt.

These pyramids, built by the ancient Egyptians more than four thousand years ago, stand in modern-day Giza, Egypt. Mayan pyramids reminded many people of Egyptian pyramids.

He insists that they were native to Mexico and Central America.

Thanks to this adventurous writer from New York, people around the world are learning about the splendors of an ancient civilization in Latin America. Stephens's book inspires scholars to study Palenque and other ruins in Mexico and Central America.

"Here were the remains of a cultivated, polished, and peculiar people, who had . . . reached their golden age, and perished, entirely unknown. The links which connected them to the human family were severed and lost, and [the ruins] were the only memorials of their footsteps upon earth."

—John Stephens, 1853

In 1949 Albert Ruz Lhuillier became the leader of a team of archaeologists who would attempt to unravel the mysteries at Palenque. The structure pictured above became known as the Temple of Inscriptions. It was named for the hieroglyphic tablets discovered there by Stephens and Catherwood more than one hundred years earlier.

CHAPTER two
THE HIDDEN STAIRCASE

In 1949—more than one hundred years after Stephens and Catherwood's voyage—a bright and enthusiastic Mexican archaeologist arrives at Palenque. Alberto Ruz Lhuillier is the new leader of the excavations (digging) at the ruin. Mexico's National Institute of Anthropology and History is sponsoring the work with money from Nelson Rockefeller. The Rockefellers are one of the wealthiest families in the United States.

By this time, scholars have identified the people who built Palenque. They were the ancient Maya, who also built Copán in Honduras and many other cities in the region. Descendants of the ancient Maya still live in Mexico and Central America. They are very proud of their heritage.

Ruz is excited to be working at Palenque. As an archaeologist, he thinks of himself as a detective. He looks for hidden clues in the places he studies. Maybe he will make a great discovery here.

First, the archaeologist and his staff build a house for themselves near the ruins. Among Ruz's workers is his brother Miguel, who is an artist.

Next, the men start clearing away the trees strangling the stone buildings. Some of the trees are valuable. The mahogany makes fine furniture. The sapote's sap is a key ingredient in chewing gum. These trees have contributed unexpectedly to learning about the Maya. Some men who have hunted in the jungle for the sapote have discovered Mayan ruins.

Ruz needs to decide where in Palenque he wants to begin exploring. He won't be spending his time in the palace. Thirty years earlier, the Mexican government hired an American archaeologist to excavate and restore it.

Palenque's other buildings include eight temples sitting on pyramids. There are also ball courts, where the adult Mayas played soccerlike games.

"To us, a [piece of pottery] is as vital a clue as the cigarette stub left by a criminal; the broken edge of a stucco floor may be as significant as a fingerprint."

—Alberto Ruz Lhuillier, 1953

Below is the ball court at Palenque. The game was similar to soccer. Each of two opposing teams tried to make a goal with a heavy rubber ball. The players kept the ball in the air with the head and upper body. They were not allowed to hit it with their hands or their legs.

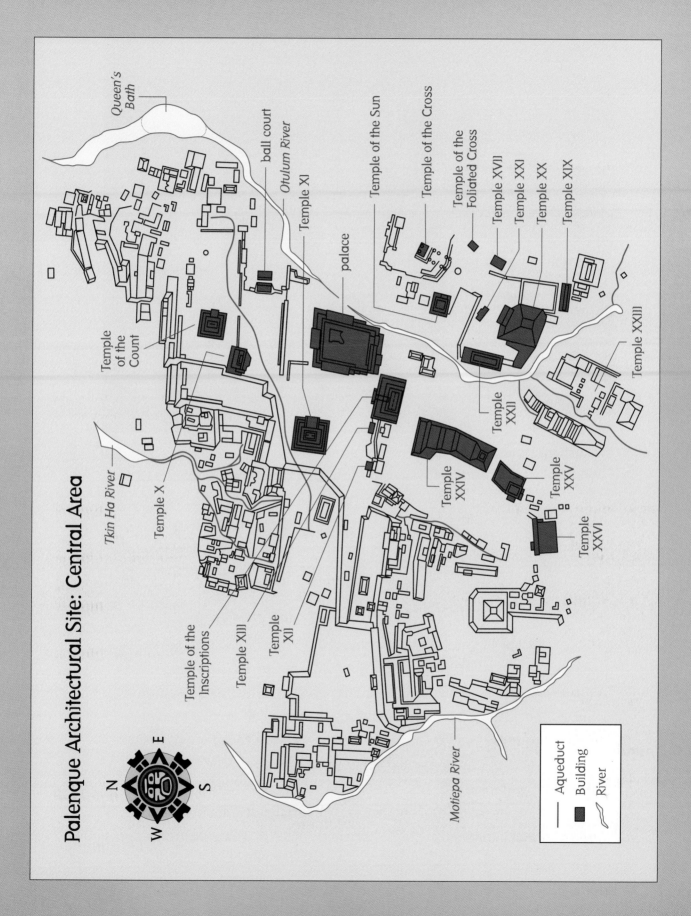

Palenque Architectural Site: Central Area

N E S W

Queen's Bath

ball court

Otulum River

Temple XI

Temple of the Sun

Temple of the Cross

Temple of the Foliated Cross

Temple XVII

Temple XXI

Temple XX

Temple XIX

palace

Temple XXII

Temple XXIII

Temple of the Count

Tkin Ha River

Temple X

Temple XXIV

Temple XXV

Temple XXVI

Temple of the Inscriptions

Temple XIII

Temple XII

Motiepa River

Aqueduct

Building

River

This reconstruction of the tomb of ancient Egypt's King Tutankhamen (1370–1352 B.C.) shows the gold and treasures discovered there by archaeologists in 1922. Ruz may have hoped for an equally exciting find in Palenque.

Ruz decides to investigate the temple atop the tallest pyramid. One reason this pyramid interests him is its height. The pyramid is so tall that it is visible from the modern village of Palenque, which is about 5 miles (8 km) away.

Maya scholars cannot help wondering whether the Maya buried some of their great leaders inside pyramids, as the Egyptians did. In 1922 a British archaeologist discovered the tomb of ancient Egypt's King Tutankhamen inside a pyramid. The gold-filled tomb created a lot of excitement around the world.

Ruz may have that famous discovery in the back of his mind, but he does not expect to dig up anything that dramatic. No one has ever found a tomb in a Mayan pyramid.

Ruz is interested in the temple too. The temple has not been explored thoroughly since Stephens and Catherwood's visit. It might contain some undiscovered sculptures or other interesting objects. And Ruz knows that it contains the three tablets of hieroglyphs discovered by that pair of explorers. Together the tablets contain one of the longest series of Mayan glyphs known to exist. Because of these important tablets, Ruz and his colleagues call the building that houses them the Temple of the Inscriptions.

Scholars have learned to read a few of the glyphs. These glyphs seem to be about important dates. Most experts have concluded that the entire text on all three tablets is about the Mayan calendar, astronomy, and mathematical calculations. Ruz agrees.

THE UNUSUAL FLOOR

On most days, Ruz and his workers are the only people at Palenque. Over the years, a few archaeologists have come to explore its crumbling stone buildings and pyramids. But almost no tourists visit.

Some workers clear away trees and brush from the great pyramid. Others clean the floor of the temple.

This floor greatly interests Ruz. All the other buildings in Palenque have stucco floors. The Temple of the Inscriptions has a flagstone floor. The stones fit together perfectly, like pieces of a jigsaw puzzle.

These Mayan glyphs were found in the Temple of the Inscriptions. Scholars hoped to crack the Mayan written code to find out more about the lives and times of the ancient Maya.

One of the flagstones in the temple's floor seemed out of the ordinary. Beneath it, Ruz's team unearthed a staircase descending into the pyramid.

One of the flagstones is different from the rest. It has two rows of holes on opposite sides. The holes are sealed with removable stone plugs. A few of the plugs are missing—probably taken by curious visitors.

Soon another unusual feature catches Ruz's attention. He notices that the walls do not end at the floor. Why is that?

AN EXCITING FIND

Ruz wants to know what is under the floor. Someone lifts the flagstone with the holes. Ruz and his crew begin to dig underneath it. They spend hours removing stones and dirt.

"I began to clear the floor near the slab and to remove the dirt—and it was then that I found the cigarette butt of the criminal, the architectural detail that gave a certain clue: the walls of the temple continued beneath the floor, proving that originally some construction on a lower level was connected with the temple."

—Alberto Ruz Lhuillier, 1953

Then someone's shovel strikes a horizontal stone beam. When the men remove the dirt around the beam, they can see that it is about 1 foot (0.3 m) thick and 6 feet (1.8 m) long. The beam connects two sloping walls. Ruz guesses that he and his workers have uncovered a space with an arched ceiling. The beam is near the top of the ceiling.

"Next morning at breakfast we discussed the purpose of the stairway; each of us had a different suggestion. My brother Miguel, one of our artists, jokingly called it a fire escape."

—Alberto Ruz Lhuillier, 1953

The men continue digging 6 feet (1.8 m) below the flagstone floor. It is hard work, but they find their reward. They uncover a step made from stone slabs and stucco. Ruz realizes that his crew has reached a stairway under an arched ceiling. It leads down into the pyramid! No one has ever found something like this under a Mayan temple. Ruz is determined to keep digging to the end of the stairway.

A hidden stairway winds down into the depths of the Temple of the Inscriptions. Many months of hard digging lie ahead for Ruz's team. Where will this stairway lead and what mysteries will it reveal?

CHAPTER three
DUST, DIRT, AND RUBBLE

The buried stairway opens a new chapter in the mystery of the Temple of the Inscriptions. Like any good detective, Ruz just has to find out what this clue means.

The archaeologist works alongside about eight other men. They come from nearby villages and from the Yucatán region, which lies northeast of Palenque. Ruz guesses these men are all distantly related to the ancient Maya who built the temple and pyramid.

The work season is short. It runs from April to July because those are the driest months. For most of the year, Palenque gets daily rain. Lots of rain creates mud, which makes digging impossible. Ruz hopes he and his men will solve the mystery of the stairway before they must leave Palenque for the year.

They make very slow progress. Some of the men dig while others haul out the dirt and rocks with buckets, ropes, and pulleys.

The stairway is dark, so Ruz and the workers light it with a gas lamp. Unfortunately, the lamp burns up valuable oxygen and gives off a lot of heat. The only fresh air in the stairway comes from the top of the hole they're digging. Dust and humidity add to the men's misery.

As they slowly clear out the stairs, the archaeologist notices an unusual feature. A square tube made of small, flat stones runs along the wall. Maybe he'll figure out what it is when he discovers what lies at the bottom of the stairs.

When it is time to leave in July, Ruz does not feel his crew has accomplished enough. The men have uncovered only twenty-three stairs.

Ruz tries to guess where the stairway leads. Maybe it is connected to other rooms in the temple. Or it could be a secret passage to another temple. There is another possibility too—a very exciting one. Maybe there is actually a tomb in the pyramid.

The square tube running along the wall in the stairway can be seen on the left side of the stair in this photo.

ENDLESS STAIRS

Ruz and his workers begin their second season, in 1950, with an improvement. They set up an electric light over the stairs. It does not use up precious oxygen, and it's much cooler too. But working conditions are still unpleasant. In fact, as the men descend deeper into the pyramid, there is less and less oxygen to breathe.

After Ruz and his crew uncover twenty-three more stairs, they arrive at a landing. There the stairs take a U-turn and head down toward the center of the pyramid. But the men must stop once again because the rain is growing too heavy. Ruz promises that when they return the following April, they will surely discover where the stairs are leading them.

The third spring, in 1951, Ruz discovers ventilation shafts in the ceiling above the stairs. They run horizontally through the thick pyramid wall. At first Ruz thinks the shafts are secret tunnels. After the men clear the rocks plugging the "tunnels," he realizes what they are. Working conditions get much better. Suddenly they have fresh air and good light coming from the courtyard to the west.

As the men dig deeper, the rocks are harder to remove. They are heavier, and time has cemented them together. Over the centuries, lime has seeped out of the limestone and then hardened into a natural mortar.

Ruz thinks the ancient Maya plugged the stairway with heavy rocks so that no one could possibly find whatever they'd placed at the bottom. But what could be so precious?

"It's a simple matter to roll rocks down a stairway and jam it full, but to hoist them out again, rock by rock and bucketful by bucketful—that is a different story."

—Alberto Ruz Lhuillier, 1953

By the end of the third season, the men have cleared only thirteen more stairs. But Ruz knows they are almost at the level of the plaza outside. When they reach that level, he believes the stairs will end. He doesn't think the stairs continue underground. The next season, the men will have

Ruz inside the Temple of the Inscriptions. His team worked for months uncovering the staircase that led deep into the pyramid.

to clear only another 10 feet (3 m) of rubble to find out what lies at the bottom of the stairs.

Ruz assures everyone that they will certainly solve their mystery next year. One worker smiles. "How many episodes has this 'whodunnit' of yours?" he asks.

TWO WALLS AND TWO BOXES

As Ruz leaves home for Palenque in spring of 1952, his wife warns him not to return until he solves the mystery inside the pyramid below the Temple of the Inscriptions. She is joking, but Ruz hopes this will indeed be his last season of digging. Two other archaeologists, César Sáenz and Rafael Orellana, are assisting him this season.

Ruz and the crew quickly remove the dirt and rubble from the last twelve steps. There are seventy-one steps all together, and it has taken more than three seasons to clear them! But the men face still more obstacles.

At the bottom of the stairs they see a wall made of packed stones. After the men take apart the wall, they find themselves standing in a hallway, facing another, stronger-looking wall. In front of it is a box made from stone slabs joined with mortar.

Ruz guesses the box might contain precious objects that the Maya left as offerings to their gods. He opens it eagerly and discovers seven jade beads and two flower-shaped jade earplugs. The box also contains three shells painted red. The most beautiful item in it is a teardrop-shaped pearl earring 0.5 inch (1.3 cm) long.

These treasures give everyone a much-needed boost. Ruz notes the discoveries and removes the box.

Next, the men must attack the second wall. It fills the hallway completely, from top to bottom and side to side. In this wall, the stones have been cemented together by men, not by nature.

Ruz's team discovered jade ornaments (*below)* and red-painted shells (*left)* inside a box at the base of the stairs inside the pyramid. The artifacts are on display at the National Museum of Anthropology and History in Mexico City.

Ruz hopes that when the crew breaks through the wall, they will finally know what the Maya were hiding. It takes them a week of hard labor. In fact, it is the hardest work they have done since they first came to Palenque. The wall is more than 12 feet (3.7 m) thick.

When the men finally break through the wall, they find yet another box. This one is larger than the first. Ruz expects to find another offering of jewels. Maybe they will be even more beautiful.

The contents of the box sadden everyone. Inside are the skeletons of

This skeleton is one of six Ruz and his team found at the bottom of the stairway beneath the Temple of the Inscriptions.

Blood Sacrifice

The Maya believed in many gods. They thought these gods needed human blood for nourishment. To help the gods and also to win their favor, they sometimes sacrificed human blood. Killing people was an extreme way to make a blood sacrifice. Mayan kings and important people also sacrificed their own blood to please their gods. They pricked their skin or tongues and used paper to absorb the blood. Then they burned the paper. This ritual was called bloodletting.

Prisoners await their death during a human sacrifice. This scene is in a mural found in the ancient Mayan city of Bonampak in modern-day Mexico.

six young people. Ruz again records the discoveries and removes the box from the pyramid.

He wonders whether they will find anything else. Did they work more than three seasons only to uncover a few jewels and anonymous human skeletons?

Ruz's team came upon a second wall at the end of the hallway. When they were finally able to remove all of its stones, they discovered a chamber with a carved limestone slab and dripping with stalactites and stalagmites. Ruz is photographed here inside the chamber.

CHAPTER four

A GREAT DISCOVERY

Ruz and his men are standing at the end of the hallway at the pyramid's center, beyond the second stone wall. The sloping walls before them and to their right seem solid. Have they come to the end of their journey?

Maybe not. There is some rubble in front of the wall to their left. They begin removing it. They notice a large triangular object lodged in the wall. As they continue to clear the debris, one worker pokes his crowbar into the rubble beside the triangle. He cries out. He was expecting to hit rock, but there is nothing behind the rubble—just air.

Ruz thinks there may be a room behind this wall. He feels sure his crew is about to solve the mystery of the hidden stairway. Ruz asks the worker to remove a stone from the spot he poked with his crowbar.

Ruz's heart is pounding as he enlarges the opening and slides a lightbulb through it. Then he looks through the hole. The sight takes his breath away.

Ruz sees a room that looks like an ice sculpture. Its sparkling walls, stalactites, and stalagmites dazzle him. The stalactites look like delicate icicles hanging from the ceiling. Ruz knows they formed when water seeped into the room, combined with lime from the limestone, and dripped from the ceiling. Growing up from the floor are stalagmites, formed in a similar

> "Out of the dim shadows emerged a vision from a fairy tale, a fantastic ethereal sight from another world. . . . As I gazed in awe and astonishment, I described the marvelous sight to my colleagues, César Sáenz and Rafael Orellana, but they wouldn't believe me until they pushed me aside and had seen with their own eyes the fascinating spectacle."
> —Alberto Ruz Lhuillier, 1953

way from dripping water. The stalagmites remind Ruz of wax drippings from giant candles.

Ruz continues to peer through the small hole. He notices that large stucco sculptures of people decorate the walls. Then he looks at the floor again. There he sees something far more interesting than stalagmites.

A large rectangular stone slab takes up most of the floor. Ruz can see red hieroglyphs painted on the sides

Nine stucco figures, such as the one at right, decorate the walls of the chamber Ruz discovered behind the wall. Ruz believed they are priests.

The Hidden Staircase

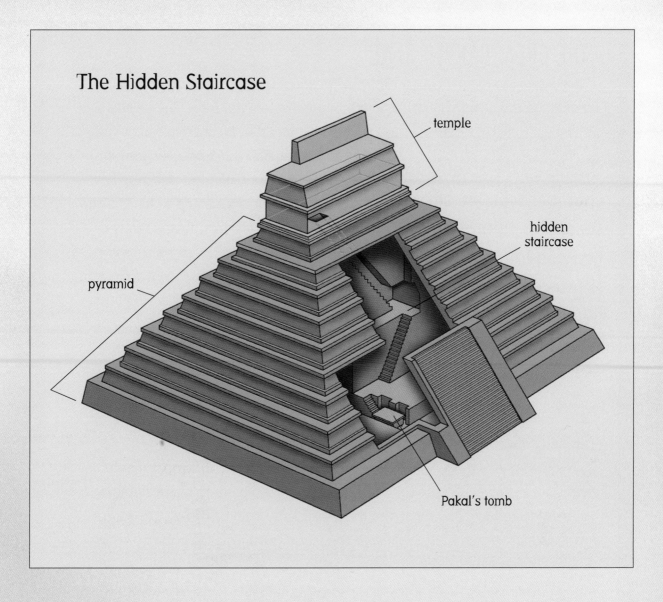

temple

hidden staircase

pyramid

Pakal's tomb

of the slab. Although he does not have a good view of the top, he can tell it has carved images on it.

The archaeologist and his crew cannot wait to enter the room, but wait they must. The triangular object in the wall is a huge stone, and it is blocking the room's entrance. It is about 8 feet (2.4 m) high and 1 foot (0.3 m) thick.

For two days, the men strain to move the great stone with pulleys and levers. Ruz guesses that it weighs several tons. Eventually the men manage to move the stone enough so a person can walk through the entrance.

THE GREAT CARVED SLAB

Ruz enters the room on June 15, 1952. He imagines the ancient people who last stood there and wishes he could communicate with them. The archaeologist is glad that he and his crew worked so hard to find this place. He knows it was worth four seasons of labor.

> "I entered the mysterious chamber with the strange sensation natural for the first one to tread the entrance steps in a thousand years."
>
> —Alberto Ruz Lhuillier, 1953

After losing himself in his thoughts for a while, Ruz is ready to get back to work. He and his crew stay in the room from eleven o'clock in the morning until midnight. They photograph the richly dressed stucco people on the wall, whom Ruz believes are priests. And they measure the room, which is larger than most Mayan rooms. It is about 29 feet (8.8 m) long and 13 feet (4 m) wide. The arched ceiling is very high—about 23 feet (7 m) above the floor.

Ruz spends most of his time in this room studying the great carved slab. He believes it is the top of an altar that was used by Mayan priests. It is more than half as wide as the room and almost half as long. The altar is in excellent condition. Ruz can see the pictures and hieroglyphs carved in its limestone very clearly.

In the middle of the altar's top surface is a picture of a man. Ruz believes the man is important. He is wearing a lot of jewelry and a fancy headdress. The man looks as if he is sitting back or falling. Right below him is the mask of an earth monster. According to Mayan beliefs, people descended into the underworld through the open mouth of this monster.

Above the man is a complex picture that looks like a cross. It is a Mayan tree of life. A two-headed serpent winds around its two main

Tree of Life

The Maya believed Earth was flat and had four corners. They thought that a tree of life stood at each corner and supported it, just as a pillar supports a building's roof.

The stone slab in the underground room is covered with elaborate carvings and glyphs. Ruz believed the slab depicts ancient Mayan beliefs about death.

branches. On top of the tree sits a bird called a quetzal, which the Maya believed was magical. A frame of glyphs surrounds the entire picture. Ruz recognizes the symbols for Venus, the sun, and the moon, so he knows these are astronomical glyphs.

Ruz believes the man in the picture knows he must die and go to the underworld. But the man is gazing up at the tree of life. He is hoping that after his death, he will soon leave the underworld and be reborn in an afterlife. Ruz believes the sun, moon, and Venus represent the universe that surrounds all humans.

Running along the vertical sides of the limestone slab are fifty-four hieroglyphs.

"Can you read that writing, chief?" a worker asks.

"Only the dates," Ruz replies. He believes one glyph says A.D. 603 and another says January 27, A.D. 633. January 27 happens to be Ruz's birthday.

TIME TO LEAVE

Ruz believes he has solved the great mystery beneath the Temple of the Inscriptions. The room he is standing in was a very holy place used by Mayan priests. Their altar is a beautifully carved masterpiece of Mayan art.

Great Record Keepers

The Maya were the first people in the Americas to keep records of their history. They recorded important events on temple walls, on large monuments, and even on their pottery *(below)*.

Ruz is not quite finished studying this room, though. He notices that the altar does not sit on the floor. It rests on a huge stone block. That lower block sits on six large stones. The archaeologist wants to know whether there is something in the giant block under the carved slab.

Ruz wants to stay in Palenque, but he knows he must leave. Frequent rain seeps into the room. Water runs down the stalactites. It is an uncomfortably damp place to work. He plans to return in the middle of November, when there will be a bit less rain.

In this decorated vase, attendants transport their ruler in a litter (portable chair). Attendants and a dog accompany him.

Ruz and his team uncovered more mysteries about Palenque when they lifted the carved stone slab and revealed what appeared to be a stone sarcophagus (coffin).

CHAPTER five

THE ALTAR IS
NOT REALLY
AN ALTAR

True to his plan, Ruz returns to Palenque in the middle of November 1952. Five months was a long time to wait for another visit to the room inside the pyramid.

This time Ruz and his crew bring an auger, a tool for drilling holes. They plan to drill into the giant stone block below the altar's carved slab. If the block is hollow, the men will know that something is probably inside it.

Nothing about this dig in Palenque is quick or easy—not even drilling a hole! Just like every other task the crew has undertaken, this one is slow and difficult. Drilling through rock is boring too.

After a few days, the moment Ruz has been hoping for finally arrives. The auger meets no more resistance. So the big stone block must be hollow.

Ruz tries looking through the drilled hole. He can see something red, but he has no idea what it is. He does know one thing: The carved slab is not an altar after all. It is a lid for a huge stone container. To look inside, the men will have to raise the slab. The archaeologist guesses that it weighs about 5 tons (4.5 metric tons).

JACKING UP THE GREAT SLAB

The men will have to lift the carved slab very carefully, so it does not crack. They have four metal builder's jacks (tools for lifting heavy objects). To place the jacks at the right height, Ruz and his crew will need to set them on some strong, short logs.

On November 27, the men begin the day at six o'clock in the morning. They have a lot of hard work to do. They go into the forest to search for *bari* trees, which have very strong wood. They cut down some of these trees and saw four short, wide logs from the trunks. Then they haul the logs back to the pyramid and up its steps. Inside the Temple of the Inscriptions, they lower the logs with ropes down the secret stairway.

The carved slab is wider and longer than the hollow stone block under it. Beneath each corner of the slab, the men set a jack on one bari log. The logs steady and support the jacks.

The crew is finally ready to raise the carved lid, and Ruz is very excited. He has completely lost track of time and does not really care.

The head of his crew, Augustín Alvarez, knows the time. "Six o'clock, [boss]," he says. "And the men have worked twelve hours without eating."

Augustín thinks it is time to quit for the day. Ruz cannot bear the thought of stopping. He tells Augustín to send for some tortillas, beans, and coffee. After eating their dinner, the men are ready to jack up the carved slab.

A man stands at each corner of the slab. Together they slowly raise it with the jacks. Each time they lift it 1 inch (2.5 cm), someone slips a wooden board under it. That way if a jack slips, the slab will not fall and crack.

When the men have raised the slab a few inches, Ruz can see what lies beneath it. There is another stone lid. This one is smooth and shaped like a bell. At each end are two round holes with stone plugs. The holes are similar to the ones in the temple flagstone that covered the stairway.

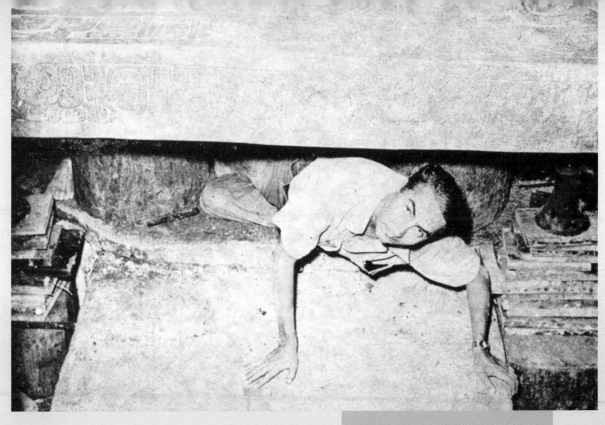

Ruz peered out from beneath the great stone slab, which had been propped up on blocks of wood so the crew could reveal what lay underneath.

Ruz knows the Maya made the holes so they could lift this lid.

The men continue lifting the carved slab inch by inch. Everyone is tense with excitement. When they have raised the slab about 15 inches (38 cm), Ruz says suddenly, "I can't wait any longer, boys. Here I go!" He slips underneath the carved slab.

Ruz removes the plugs from the four holes in the smooth lid. He shines his flashlight through one hole and looks through another.

ANOTHER GREAT DISCOVERY

At first the archaeologist sees a blur of green, red, and white. Gradually the objects in the great stone block come into focus. Ruz sees jade jewelry, bones, and some teeth painted red. There are pieces of a broken mask too. Ruz has found an ancient stone coffin, called a sarcophagus. It is the first sarcophagus a modern archaeologist has ever found in a Mayan pyramid! The men quickly remove the smooth stone lid so Ruz can study the contents of the coffin. The inside is a big hole carved out of the giant stone block. It is painted red.

Ruz looks over the skeleton, which is male. He guesses that the man was between forty and fifty years old and taller than most ancient Maya were. The archaeologist cannot be sure of the man's height, though. He cannot measure the decayed bones properly.

Most amazing are all the jade ornaments in the coffin. Ruz thinks the Maya placed these on the man's body when they buried him. The large piece of jewelry with 189 polished jade tubes must have rested on his chest. A collar with more jade beads in different

"I was gazing at the death face of him for whom all this stupendous work—the crypt, the sculpture, the stairway, the great pyramid with its crowning temple—had been built."

—Alberto Ruz Lhuillier , 1953

A reconstruction of the room inside the base of the pyramid shows what Ruz discovered. Under the carved stone slab lay a sarcophagus. The inside of the sarcophagus is painted red, and Ruz found a human skeleton there.

shapes once encircled his neck. Some of these beads are round, others look like flowers, and still others look like the heads of snakes. Each of the man's finger bones still wears a jade ring. A jade mask once covered the man's face. The eyes of the mask are made of shell. The Maya set black stones into the shells to look like pupils.

Who was this man? Ruz knows he must have been very important. The people of Palenque would not have buried an ordinary person so grandly. The archaeologist guesses that the man was a priest.

PUTTING THE PUZZLE TOGETHER

Ruz decides the Maya built this tomb about the same time as they built the Temple of the Inscriptions. After they buried the great man, they closed off the room with the triangular rock. Then they sacrificed the young people. Finally, they filled the stairway with rubble so no one would disturb the sarcophagus.

This jade burial mask lay on the face of the body in the tomb. The mask is made of many individual pieces of jade, shell, and stone.

On the outside of the sarcophagus is the answer to another question that has been nagging Ruz. He has been wondering about that square tube running along the stairway and hallway. He sees that it starts in the shape of a hollow snake on the side of the sarcophagus. Then its shape changes to a square tube, which extends all the way up to the floor of the temple. Ruz calls it a psychic duct. The Maya believed it allowed them to communicate with the spirit of the dead man.

Although Ruz has put together many pieces of the puzzle, he is still missing an important bit of information. Like other archaeologists, he cannot read most of the glyphs on the edge of the carved slab covering the sarcophagus. Nor can he read many of the inscriptions on the three tablets in the temple above. If he could read more, he might know the identity of the great man lying inside the sarcophagus.

More than a century has passed since John Stephens and Frederick Catherwood first gazed on the tablets. But no one has broken the code to most Mayan

A reconstruction of Pakal's burial shows what the body would have looked like when it was placed in the sarcophagus.

> "Mexican pyramids always have been thought to be completely solid pedestals for the temples atop them. The Palenque discovery will give new orientation to Mexican archaeology and perhaps lead to an illumination of the mysterious development of the Mayan empire."
>
> —*New York Times*, December 5, 1952

glyphs. Was Stephens right? Does the mysterious writing tell the early history of the Maya, including the history of the man in the sarcophagus? Ruz's great discovery may encourage others to find some answers.

THE WORLD LEARNS ABOUT RUZ'S DISCOVERY

Newspapers report on Ruz's wildly successful excavation in Palenque. The world learns that the Maya buried some of their most important people in pyramids, just as the ancient Egyptians did. Once again, people discuss the similarities between Egyptian and Mayan pyramids.

But Ruz does not think his discovery will change archaeologists' ideas about how Mayan culture developed. Just like John Stephens a century earlier, Ruz believes there was no connection between the Maya and the Egyptians.

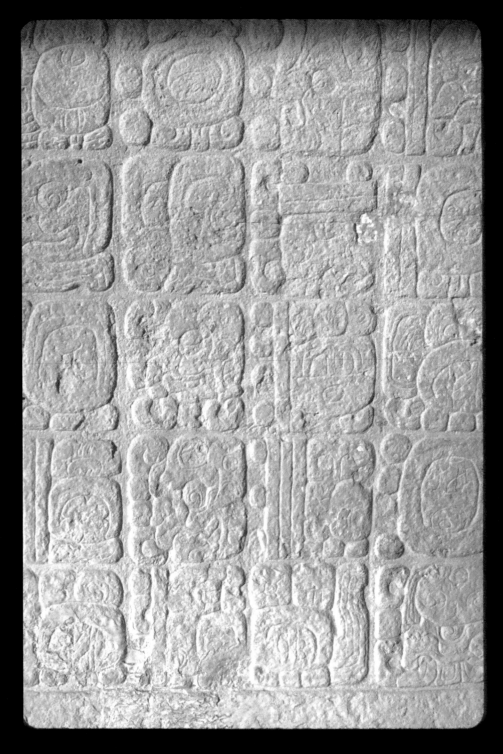

Deciphering the Mayan glyphs at the Temple of the Inscriptions enabled scholars to identify the body in the temple sarcophgus. By 1973 scholars knew that some glyphs at Palenque represent the names of Mayan cities. Other represent the names of four people, and still others stand for dates. Scholars of the twenty-first century continue to work on decoding Mayan glyphs.

CHAPTER six

THE MAN IN THE SARCOPHAGUS

In the fall of 1973, Ruz receives an invitation. A group of Maya scholars ask him to attend a small conference about the ruins of Palenque. It will take place in the modern town of Palenque.

Ruz does not go. In fact, not one Mexican or Central American Maya scholar attends this meeting. No students from the University of Mexico go either. Most of the people who attend are American experts in Mayan art, archaeology, or hieroglyphs.

Mexican and American Maya scholars do not work together as well as they once did. The country's president, Luis Echeverría Álvarez, does not like Americans. In fact, he seems eager to keep American archaeologists out of Mexico.

The president of Mexico in 1973, Luis Echeverría Álvarez, drove a wedge between Mexican and American archaeologists. His policies added to the tensions between Ruz and his colleagues from other countries.

Living History

Some Mexican people do come to the conference, but they are not scholars. On some afternoons, the conference hosts special sessions for local residents. Many of them are descendants of the ancient Maya, and they come to learn about their ancestors.

THE LAST PIECE OF THE PUZZLE

The conference begins on December 14, 1973, and lasts more than a week. One afternoon three scholars—Linda Schele, Floyd Lounsbury, and Peter Matthews—decide to work together. They plan to study the hieroglyphs in the Temple of the Inscriptions, on the sarcophagus beneath the temple, and on other buildings and monuments of ancient Palenque. The three want to figure out who the kings of Palenque were and when they ruled.

By this time, Maya experts can read more glyphs than they could when Ruz discovered the sarcophagus. In 1952 most experts could read only some dates. In 1973 scholars know that some glyphs mean the name of Mayan cities, such as Palenque. They also recognize four

Scholars and experts in Mayan art and culture gathered in a house in Palenque in 1973.

glyphs that mean the names of four different people at Palenque. But they don't know who these people were or how to say the names.

The three scholars who join forces at the conference make a very good team. Schele is an American painter who knows the Palenque ruins very well. Lounsbury, another American, has learned two Mayan languages from modern Mayan people. These are the same languages that the ancient scribes used. Modern Maya write these languages with letters, not glyphs. But just knowing the Mayan words helps Lounsbury decode glyphs. He already knows how to figure out the modern date (the A.D. year) for a Mayan date recorded on a hiero-glyph. This is tricky, because the Mayan calendar was very complex.

Merle Greene Robertson

Merle Greene Robertson is one of the main organizers of the conference. She is an American photographer and artist and also a great lover of the ruins at Palenque. Since 1964 she has been taking detailed photographs to record all the stucco and limestone sculpture there. She worries that pollution from Mexico's oil and gas industries is harming the ancient artwork. The summer before the conference, Schele worked as Robertson's lighting assistant.

Matthews, the third member of the team, is an Australian archaeology student at a Canadian university. He has arrived with valuable information. In a blue notebook, he has recorded every glyph from Palenque that carries a Mayan date.

The group of three works with lightning speed. In just a few hours, they figure out the life stories of six Palenque kings. That evening they present the information to their amazed colleagues. This is the first time scholars have managed to connect Palenque's temples and palace with the real people who lived among them more than one thousand years earlier.

No one is thinking of John Stephens at that moment. But the group of three has proven something that Stephens guessed back in 1840, when he explored the Temple of the Inscriptions. He was sure that Mayan hiero-glyphs contained the history of the Mayan people.

"That night, after dinner, the Linda and Peter show began, with Floyd acting as moderator and commentator. What they came up with was nothing less than the history of Palenque from . . . the beginning of the seventh century through the city's [end]. . . . History had been made before our very eyes."

—Michael Coe, an expert on the ancient Maya, 1992

Schele, Lounsbury, and Matthews notice that the hieroglyphs at Palenque often mention the names of two Mayan rulers. A glyph that looks like a shield represents one of these kings, so the group calls him Lord Shield. They realize that he is the great man buried in the sarcophagus beneath the Temple of the Inscriptions.

Soon after the conference, Matthew's professor David Kelley discovers that Mayan scribes did not always represent Lord Shield with the shield symbol. Sometimes they used glyphs representing parts of words, just like syllables in a modern language. This discovery helps Kelley figure out Lord Shield's real name. The king's name was Pakal!

Kelley and Lounsbury also figure out the exact years of Pakal's life. They calculate that he died when he was eighty years old.

RUZ GOES ON THE ATTACK

In 1974 Schele, Lounsbury, and Matthews publish two articles about their discoveries at the Palenque conference. These articles infuriate Ruz. The group of three contradicts Ruz's opinions, which he has explained in his own book published the year before.

Ruz insists that the shield glyph is not a symbol for the man buried in the sarcophagus. And he continues to believe the man did not live more than fifty years. He writes two articles attacking the group of three's work. However, most Maya experts agree with Schele, Lounsbury, and Matthews.

The scholars who came to the Palenque conference are much younger than Ruz. He sees them as upstarts and foreigners, even though he is not a native Mexican himself. (He was born in France.) These tensions between the different generations and nationalities are painful for everyone.

Ruz and the younger scholars do have a common goal, though. They spend a lot of their time studying ancient Mayan ruins and hieroglyphs for the same reason. They all want to uncover the lost history of an ancient people and tell it to the world. This is what archaeology is all about.

Mayan Glyphs

Below are six copies of the same square with hieroglyphic writing. It is from one of the tablets in the Temple of the Inscriptions. In the first five squares, a different glyph is highlighted. Each glyph represents one or two syllables. The square helped scholars figure out the name of the man buried in the sarcophagus. When all of the syllables are strung together, as in the final square, the man's formal name emerges. He is K'inich Janaab Pakal.

 read as K'INICH, possibly translated as "sun-faced"

 a sign for the syllable *ka*

 read as JANAAB (a type of flower)

 a sign for the syllable *la*.

 read as the syllable *pa*

 K'inich Janaab Pakal

Decades after Ruz's great find in Palenque, archaeologists still work to uncover more artifacts there.

EPILOGUE

When Alberto Ruz Lhuillier found Pakal's sarcophagus in 1952, he made one of the world's greatest modern discoveries about the ancient Maya. Suddenly archaeologists looked at Mayan pyramids differently. They realized a pyramid could be more than a base for a temple. It might contain the coffin of a king or a noble person. In the decade after Ruz's find, archaeologists discovered another royal Mayan tomb inside a pyramid in Guatemala.

Many archaeologists already admired the elegance of the Temple of the Inscriptions. But when Ruz found the hidden stairway and sarcophagus, he showed that the Maya could design and build structures that were complex as well as lovely.

Ruz's discovery was an impressive example of the ancient Maya's art, as well as their architecture and engineering. The carved lid of Pakal's sarcophagus remains one of the most beautiful known works by ancient Mayan artists.

Ruz guessed correctly that the man who lay inside the sarcophagus had directed the construction of the temple and the tomb. Scholars learned later that Pakal had begun a revolution in building techniques. During and after Pakal's reign, the Maya built lighter and more graceful buildings. The Temple of the Inscriptions was the loveliest of all.

Alberto Ruz Lhuillier died in 1979. He is buried in the tomb shown above in Palenque.

Ruz reminded scholars and Maya lovers that archaeology can be a great adventure. And he showed them how much persistence and hard, sweaty work are behind the greatest discoveries. Finally, he proved that the best archaeologists are detectives. After all, many people had walked over the flagstone that caught Ruz's eye in the Temple of the Inscriptions. But only one man decided to lift it up.

The modern world knows Palenque as one of the most stunning ancient Maya sites ever found. Every year hordes of tourists climb the

Tomb of the Red Queen

In 1994 archaeologists discovered another sarcophagus at Palenque. They found it inside the temple next door to the Temple of the Inscriptions. This neighboring temple has a stairway leading to a sealed room, just like the Temple of the Inscriptions. Inside the room, archaeologists found a sarcophagus painted red. Like Pakal's sarcophagus, this one was covered with a heavy limestone slab. The remains of a woman lay inside. So did many pieces of jade and pearl, which may have been part of a mask. Everything, including the skeleton, was covered with red powder. No one has identified this woman. Archaeologists call her the Red Queen because of the red powder.

This mask, found in the tomb of the Red Queen, was reconstructed from about 220 mosaic pieces. The pieces are mostly malachite (a green mineral), with jade and obsidian inlays to resemble the Red Queen's eyes.

steps of the pyramid to visit the Temple of the Inscriptions. Although Pakal's tomb is closed to the public, visitors can descend the long, damp stairway and they can view the sarcophagus lid. Pakal's burial mask is on display in Mexico City at the National Museum of Anthropology.

TIMELINE

2000 B.C.
Mayan civilization begins.

A.D. 290
The Classic period begins. During this period, Mayan civilization is at its peak and Mayan culture reaches its highest point of development.

615
Pakal begins ruling Palenque. He leads Palenque into a golden age, during which the city-state is at the height of its power and architectural beauty.

683
Pakal dies, and his people bury him in a sarcophagus under the Temple of the Inscriptions. Chan Bahlum becomes king.

800
The Maya have left Palenque.

900
The postclassic period begins. During this period, other Mayan city-states near Palenque, including Tikal, collapse. Remaining Mayan populations are mainly to the north and south of Palenque.

1524
Hernán Cortés, the Spanish conqueror of Mexico, passes within about 30 miles (48 km) of Palenque. He has never heard of it.

1527
The Spanish conquer the northern Maya.

1546
The Spanish conquer most of the southern Maya.

1840
John Stephens and Frederick Catherwood explore Palenque and record all that they see.

1902
The last volume of *Archaeology*, by Alfred Maudslay, is published. This work includes several volumes. They contain detailed drawings of the architecture, art, and hieroglyphs from every important ancient Mayan site. Maudslay, of Great Britain, visited them all after reading Stephens's account of his travels.

1946
Giles Healey finds murals that the ancient Maya had painted on the walls of a temple. The murals include a scene after a battle and another scene of life at a royal court. The site, called Bonampak, is 113 miles (183 km) southeast of Palenque.

1952
Alberto Ruz Lhuillier discovers a sarcophagus in the pyramid beneath the Temple of the Inscriptions.

1973
At a conference in the village of Palenque, three Maya experts decode some Palenque hieroglyphs. They discover that a king named Pakal is the man in the sarcophagus.

1994
Archaeologists discover the tomb of the Red Queen beneath the temple next door to the Temple of the Inscriptions.

2005
A team of American and Guatemalan scholars announce that they have found a column of ancient Mayan hieroglyphs. The column is at a remote site called San Bartolo in Guatemala. The glyphs are the oldest known Mayan writing and date from about 200 B.C.

PRONUNCIATION GUIDE

Alberto Ruz Lhuillier   ahl-BEHR-toh ROOZ LWEE-yay

Bonampak   bohn-ahm-PAHK

casa de piedras   KAH-sah de PYEH-drahs

Chan Bahlum   CHAHN bah-LOOM

Chiapas   CHYAH-pahs

Copán   koh-PAHN

Kan Xul   KAHN SHOOL

Pakal   Pah-KAHL

Palenque   pah-LEHN-kay

quetzal   KEHT-sahl

sapote   sah-POH-tay

sarcophagus   sahr-KAHF-ah-guhs

Yucatán   YOO-kah-tahn

GLOSSARY

archaeologist: an expert who digs around very old buildings and objects and studies them to learn about past people and their cultures

architect: a person who designs buildings

beam: a long, sturdy piece of wood or other building material used to support a roof or floor

excavate: to dig in the earth to find the remains of buildings, objects, or people

flagstone: a hard rock that splits into flat pieces, which are used for paving

glyph: a symbol in a system of picture writing

hieroglyphic writing: a writing system based on pictures and symbols

inscription: a carved or specially written message

jade: a precious green stone often used for jewelry

maize: corn

mortar: in modern times, a building material made of lime, water, sand, and cement

rubble: broken bricks and stones

sarcophagus: a stone coffin

stucco: a fine plaster

WHO'S WHO?

Frederick Catherwood was born in England in 1799. He became an artist and an architect. Like Stephens, he traveled through the Middle East studying ruins. Catherwood made detailed drawings of sculptures, buildings, and inscriptions with great skill.

He met John Stephens in London in 1836. Three years later, the two men traveled to Central America together to find ruins. They were thrilled to discover Palenque.

In addition to the books he illustrated for Stephens, Catherwood produced another book on his own. It was a collection of prints made from watercolors he had painted in Central America. The book was called *Views of Ancient Monuments in Central America, Chiapas, and Yucatan*. It was published in 1844.

Catherwood lived in San Francisco, California, in the early 1850s. There he sold supplies to people hoping to find gold during the California gold rush. In 1854, while he was traveling from London to New York, he drowned in a steamship accident in the Atlantic Ocean.

Alberto Ruz Lhuillier was born in France on January 27, 1906. He went to high school in Cuba and began his university training there. Ruz arrived in Mexico in 1935 and continued his education at the National School of Anthropology and then the National University of Mexico.

In 1940 he became an archaeologist at Mexico's National Institute of Anthropology and History. Eventually he became director of archaeological explorations for Mexico's Mayan ruins.

In 1952 Ruz discovered the coffin of Pakal, a Mayan king, in a tomb hidden in the pyramid beneath the Temple of the Inscriptions at Palenque. He researched and wrote about the Maya until shortly before he died on August 25, 1979.

The Mexican government wished to recognize Ruz's great contribution to Mayan archaeology. They gave permission for him to be buried near the Temple of the Inscriptions.

John Lloyd Stephens was born in New Jersey in 1805. He was only thirteen years old when he enrolled at Columbia University in New York. After he graduated, Stephens studied law and became a lawyer.

In 1836 Stephens traveled through the Middle East, where he discovered his love for the ruins of ancient civilizations. Three years later, he and Frederick Catherwood traveled to Central America to explore the ruins there. In May 1840, the two men spent about a month studying the ruins of Palenque.

Back in New York, Stephens wrote *Incidents of Travel in Central America, Chiapas, and Yucatan*. The book contained many fine drawings by Catherwood and became a best seller. Stephens returned to Mexico with Catherwood in the fall of 1841. In ten months, they visited forty-four Mayan sites. Stephens recorded their journey in *Incidents of Travel in Yucatan*, which was published in 1843. In 1849 Stephens became the vice president of the Panama Railroad Company. He died in 1852.

SOURCE NOTES

17 John L. Stephens, *Incidents of Travel in Central America, Chiapas, and Yucatan,* vol. 2 (New York: Harper and Brothers, 1853), 302.
23 Ibid., 343.
23 Ibid.
25 Ibid., 373.
27 Ibid., 356.
30 Alberto Ruz Lhuillier, "The Mystery of the Temple of the Inscriptions," trans. J. Alden Mason, *Archaeology*, Spring 1953, 3.
34 Ibid., 4.
35 Alberto Ruz Lhuillier, "The Mystery of the Mayan Temple," *Saturday Evening Post,* August 29, 1953, 96.
39 Ibid., 30.
40 Ibid., 96.

42 Ruz Lhuillier, "The Mystery of the Temple of the Inscriptions," 5.
46 Ruz Lhuillier, "The Mystery of the Mayan Temple," 96.
48 Ruz Lhuillier, "The Mystery of the Temple of the Inscriptions," 6.
50 Ruz Lhuillier, "The Mystery of the Mayan Temple," 98.
54 Ibid.
55 Ibid.
56 Ibid.
59 "Mayan Find Shows Egyptian Parallel," *New York Times*, December 5, 1952.
64 Michael D. Coe, *Breaking the Maya Code* (New York: Thames and Hudson, 1992), 205.

SELECTED BIBLIOGRAPHY

Coe, Michael D. *Breaking the Maya Code.* New York: Thames and Hudson, 1992.

Pohl, John M. D. *Exploring Mesoamerica.* New York: Oxford University Press, 1999.

Robertson, Merle Greene. *The Sculpture of Palenque: The Temple of the Inscriptions.* Princeton, NJ: Princeton University Press, 1983.

Ruz Lhuillier, Alberto. "The Mystery of the Mayan Temple." *Saturday Evening Post*, August 29, 1953.

———. "The Mystery of the Temple of the Inscriptions." Translated by J. Alden Mason. *Archaeology*, Spring 1953.

Schele, Linda, and David Freidel. *A Forest of Kings: The Untold Story of the Ancient Maya.* New York: William Morrow, 1990.

Stephens, John L. *Incidents of Travel in Central America, Chiapas, and Yucatan.* Vol. 2. New York: Harper and Brothers, 1853.

FURTHER READING AND WEBSITES

BOOKS

Day, Nancy. *Your Travel Guide to Ancient Mayan Civilization.* Minneapolis: Twenty-First Century Books, 2001.

Hamilton, Janice. *Mexico in Pictures.* Minneapolis: Twenty-First Century Books, 2003.

Kirwan, Anna. *Lady of Palenque, Flower of Bacal: Mesoamerica, A.D. 749.* New York: Scholastic, 2004.

Lourie, Peter. *The Mystery of the Maya: Uncovering the Lost City of Palenque.* Honesdale, PA: Boyds Mills Press, 2001.

Stuart, Gene S., and George E. Stuart. *Lost Kingdoms of the Maya.* Washington, DC: National Geographic Society, 1993.

Sutton, Ann, and Myron Sutton. *Among the Maya Ruins: The Adventures of John Lloyd Stephens and Frederick Catherwood.* Skokie, IL: Rand McNally, 1967.

WEBSITES

Foundation for the Advancement of Mesoamerican Studies
http://www.famsi.org. This site is loaded with information and images from many ancient cultures of Mexico and Central America, including Palenque and other Mayan cities.

Lost King of the Maya
http://www.pbs.org/wgbh/nova/maya. This site is a companion to a *NOVA* television program that aired in 2001. The site focuses on archaeologists who are using recent excavations and translations of Mayan glyphs to understand the early history of the ancient Mayan city of Copán.

Palenque Project
http://www.mesoweb.com/palenque. This site provides fascinating details about past and present investigations at Palenque, as well as stunning photos.

INDEX

ABOUT THE AUTHOR

Deborah Kops has written more than a dozen books for children and young adults, including *Ancient Rome*. She enjoys visiting historic sites in Greater Boston, where she lives with her husband and son.

PHOTO ACKNOWLEDGMENTS

The images in this book are used with the permission of: © Danny Lehman/ CORBIS, p. 4; © Scala/Art Resource, NY, p. 6; © Roy Anderson/National Geographic Society Image Collection, p. 7; © Laura Westlund/Independent Picture Service, pp. 9, 12, 31, 47, 65; Drawing by Frederick Catherwood, reproduced from Incidents of Travel in Central America, Chiapas, and Yucatan, by John L. Stephens, p. 10; 2A-13029, Photo by Stuart Rome, American Museum of Natural History Library, p. 11; © age fotostock/SuperStock, p. 13; © Newberry Library/SuperStock, pp. 14-15, 18-19, 24; The Art Archive/Gianni Dagli Orti, p. 16; © Macduff Everton/CORBIS, p. 17; The Art Archive/National Anthropological Museum Mexico/Gianni Dagli Orti, pp. 20, 49, 56, 58; © Robert Frerck/Stone/Getty Images, p. 21 (top); © Sylvia Cordaiy Photo Library Ltd/Alamy, p. 21 (bottom); Photographs by Linda Schele, © David Schele, courtesy Foundation for the Advancement of Mesoamerican Studies, Inc., www.famsi.org, pp. 22, 23, 30, 34, 36, 46, 60; Courtesy of Barnaby Rudge Booksellers ABAA, Ed Postal, p. 26; © David Sutherland/The Image Bank/Getty Images, p. 27; © Kenneth Garrett/National Geographic/Getty Images, p. 28; The Art Archive/Pharaonic Village Cairo/Gianni Dagli Orti, p. 32; © D. Donne Bryant/DDB Stock Photography, p. 33; © Justin Kerr, K8516, p. 38; Universidad Nacional Autónoma De México, Instituto De Investigaciones Filológicas, Centro De Estudios Mayas, México, pp. 40, 44, 55; © George and Audrey DeLange, p. 41 (both); © imagebroker/Alamy, p. 42; © SEF/Art Resource, NY, p. 43; © Justin Kerr, K6317, pp. 50–51; © Atlantide Phototravel/CORBIS, p. 52; © Werner Forman/Art Resource, NY, p. 57; AP Photo, p. 61; Merle Greene Robertson Archives, p. 62; AP Photo/Eduardo Verdugo, p. 66; © E & E Image Library/HIP/The Image Works, p. 68; © Janet Schwartz/AFP/Getty Images, p. 69.

Front Cover: © Kenneth Garrett/Woodfin Camp/Time & Life Pictures/Getty Images.